19-S990005022762-488-2

Printed and bound in India

PRANAVA BOOKS
INDIA

THE

SECRETS OF ANGLING.

By J[OHN] D[ENNYS] Esquire.

1613.

A REPRINT, WITH INTRODUCTION,

By THOMAS WESTWOOD.

INTRODUCTION.

THE English poets of the Art of Angling perplex us neither with their multitude, nor their magnitude. To some three or four of them may be assigned a place—shall we say midway, by courtesy?—on the ledges of Parnassus; the rest are innocent of all altitudes whatsoever, except those of Grub-street garrets, or the stilts of an absurd vanity.

Foremost among the select few, by right of seniority, and perhaps by poetic right as well, we have "I. D.," who in the cool dawn of the seventeenth century, and when the Elizabethan men were passing, one by one, into the shadow, "sang to the echo," (for he seems to have had no other audience in his own day and generation,) these "Secrets of Angling," himself being destined to become a greater secret than any he revealed.

His publisher, "R. J." (Roger Jackson) states, in his dedication of the poem to Mr. John Harborne of Tackley, that the author "intended to have printed it in his life, but was prevented by death." Other motives of reticence, however, besides that final one, may have had their weight; some faintness of heart, for instance, and some wisdom of discretion. The epoch was a trying one for the minor muse. The Elizabethan bards, as I have said, were dying out, but the national air still vibrated to their divine singing—the national heart was still at fever-heat, with "Fairy Queens," and "Passionate Pilgrims," with "heavenly Unas," and heroic "Lucreces." It would scarcely have been strange, if a poet unknown to fame, had recoiled from bringing into competition with these and such as these, a simple song of bleak and bream. But whatever the real motive may have been, I. D. of a surety closed his eyes on all the shows of this world, if not a "mute," at least an "inglorious" poet, and unconsoled,

B

perchance, by the conviction, that his modest rhymes would be brought into favour and acceptance, at a fitting time.

In 1613, appeared the first edition (12mo.), a pocket volume, with the following title: "The Secrets of Angling. Teaching, the choisest Tooles, Baytes and Seasons, for the taking of any Fish, in Pond or Riuer: practised and familiarly opened in three Bookes. By I. D. Esquire. Printed at London, for *Roger Jackson*, and are to be sould at his shop neere Fleetstreet Conduit, 1613."

In this title is an allegorical wood-cut, representing two men, one treading on a serpent, and with a sphere at the end of his angle, and over his rod a label with this inscription:

> "Hold hooke and line
> Then all is mine."

The other figure has a fish on his hook, and is labelled thus:

> "Well fayre the pleasure
> That brings such treasure."

At the back of the title is a copy of verses. "In due praise of his praise-worthy skill and worke," signed "Jo Dauies," followed by the dedication we have before alluded to, and which is given with the present reprint.

It is difficult to fix with any certainty, the number of copies extant of this edition. The Bodleian possesses one, Mr. Denison another, and Mr. Huth a third. There are also some imperfect copies.

Of the second edition [1] there is, I believe, but one known copy, which is now in the Denison collection. It is supposed (for the date is cut off) to have appeared about 1620. It was edited by W. Lauson, and the title-page states that it is "augmented with many approved experiments." Lauson's additions to the work are an address "To the reader," and some notes and recipes.

Lauson's address "To the Reader" ran thus:

"It may seeme in me presumption to adde this little comment to the work

---

[1] "Printed at London for Roger Jackson and are to be sould—" the rest cut off.

of so worthy an author. But Mr. Harrison the stationers request and desire to give his country satisfaction, must be satisfied, and in it myselfe rest excused. What mine observations are, I refer to censure : assuredly the truth stands on so well grounded experience, that but my haste, nothing can do them injury. What to me *is* doubtful, I have, as I can, explained ; what wants, in my judgement, I have supplied as the time would suffer ; what I passe by, I approve. The author by verse hath expressed much learning, and by his Answer to the Objection, shewn himselfe to have been vertuous. The subject itselfe is honest, and pleasant, and sometimes profitable. Use it, and give God all glory. Amen."

In the subsequent issues no important alteration, that I am aware of, was made either in the poem or the notes.

The third edition bore date 1630,[1] and the only known copy is in the Denison collection. A new wood-cut is used of the same subject, but badly executed. One motto is the same—the other reads : " Well fare the pleasure that yields such treasure." The fourth appeared in 1652.[2] Several copies of the latter are extant, of which two are in the British Museum and one in the possession of Mr. Denison. The woodcut here figures as a frontispiece and its place in the title is filled with the bookseller's mark, " The Hare and Sun."

The poem was reprinted *in extenso,* from the preceding edition, in Sir Egerton Brydges' " British Bibliographer,"[3] and a hundred copies, with index and short advertisement, were struck off separately. It was also noticed, with large citations, in the same *bibliophile's* " Censura Literaria"[4] in an article which was appropriated by Daniel, in the supplement to his " Rural Sports," in 1813.

The fact of the second, third, and fourth editions being distinct, is proved (if any proof were wanting) by the variations both in the title and in the leaf containing the mystical recipe—" Wouldst thou take fish ? " Thus in the second edition we are told—

" This excellent recipe you may buy ready and truely made at the signe

---

[1] " Printed in 8vo. for John Jackson in the Strand, at the sign of the Parote, 1630."

[2] " London, printed by T. H., for John Harrison, and are to be sold by Francis Coles at his shop at Old Bayley, 1652."

[3] 1812, Vol. II. p. 465.

[4] 1809, Vol. X. p. 286.

of the Black Lyon an Apothecaries', in Paule's-Churchyard neare the Great South dore."

In the third, we are referred for the same to the "Signe of the Flying Horse an Apothecaries' in Carter Lane."

While the fourth informs us that "This excellent receipt, divers Anglers can tell where you may buy them."

Beloe, speaking of the edition of 1652, says, "Perhaps there does not exist in the circle of English literature a rarer book than this." He seems to have ignored the former editions—though how this could have been with Lauson's "Augmented" in the title page, is not clear.

Pickering, in his "Bibliotheca Piscatoria" (1836) also ignores the second and third editions, but rectifies the omission in some MS. addenda to his list, which were once in my possession.

That Mr. Bohn should have been guilty of the same short-coming in his recent reprint of Lowndes, is less excusable, as the fact had become patent to any diligent seeker.

In summing up the editions, we must not omit Mr. Arber's re-issue in his "English Garner," Vol. I. (1877).

The authorship of the "Secrets" remained a vexed question until a comparatively recent period (we believe about 1811). It was attributed by Walton to Jo. Davors, Esq., several verses of the poem being quoted, with variations that were not improvements, in his "Compleat Angler." R[obert] H[owlett], in his preface to the "Angler's Sure Guide," (1706) assigns it to Dr. Donne, whom he styles "that great practitioner, master and patron of Angling," and he adds, "indeed, his seems to be the best foundation of all superstructures of this kind, and upon that basis chiefly have I raised mine."

To one or other of the six poets of the name of Davies, the poem has also been ascribed ; but all these conflicting hypotheses were finally set aside by the discovery, in the Registers of the Stationers' Company, of the following entry :—

"1612, Feb. 28th.[1] Mr. Roger Jackson entered for his copie under th'andes of Mr. Mason and Mr. Warden Hooper, a booke called the Secrets of Angling,

[1] According to others, March 23rd.

teaching the choycest tooles, baites and seasons for the taking of any fish in pond or river, praktised and opened in three bookes, by John Dennys, Esquire. vjd."

Sir Harris Nicolas, who, in his edition of Walton's Angler (1836) begins by asserting (very gratuitously) that the poem, "though entered in the name of Dennys, is by John Davors," adds a subsequent note of recantation : "There are strong reasons," he says, "for believing that the 'Secrets of Angling,' was not written by John Davors, but by John Dennys Esq., who was lord of the Manor of Oldbury-sur-Montem, in the County of Gloucester, between 1572 and 1608. He was a younger son of Sir Walter Dennys, of Pucklechurch, in that county, by Agnes, daughter and co-heiress of Sir Robert Davers or Danvers. It has been observed by Mr. James Williamson, that the author of the 'Secrets' speaks of the River Boyd as 'washing the cliffs of Deington and Week.' There is, in fact, a beautiful rivulet, called Boyd, which is formed by four distinct streams, rising in the parishes of Codrington, Pucklechurch, Dyrham and Toghill, in the southern part of the County of Gloucester, between Bath and Bristol, which join in Wyke or Week Street, in the parish of Alston and Wyke, near a bridge of three large arches, and thence, by the name of Boyd, descends to Avon, at Kynsham Bridge, and which river passes through the village of Pucklechurch and thence flows on to Bitton. At Alston and Wyke there are many high cliffs or rocks, and in the north Aisle of the Ancient Church of Pucklechurch is the burial place of the family of Dennys. John Dennys was resident in that neighbourhood in the year 1572, and so continued till 1608 during which interval he was lord of the manor of Oldbury-sur-montem, and of other places in the county of Gloucester."

There seems great and serious cause to doubt the accuracy of Sir Harris Nicolas's hypothesis, as given in the above extract.

I was favoured, some time since, by the Rev. H. N. Ellacombe, of Bitton, with a portion of the Dennys pedigree, showing six descents from the Sir Walter in question, and Mr. Ellacombe infers therefrom, and with great show of reason, that the real author of the poem was more probably Sir Walter's great-grandson, the John Dennys who was buried at Pucklechurch in 1609, four years, that is to say, previous to the publication of the volume.

The pedigree, as extracted, is as follows :	· ·

Sir Walter Dennys.	= Agnes, daughter and heir Robert Davers, or Danvers.
John Dennys of Pucklechurch.	= Fortune, widow of Wm. Kemys, of Newport, and daughter of Thos. Norton of Bristol.
Hugh Dennys, died 1559.	= Katherine, daughter of Edw. Trye, of Hardwick, co. of Gloucester ; died 1583, at Pucklechurch.
John Dennys, died 1609, buried at Pucklechurch.	= Elianor, or Helena, daughter of Thos. Millet, co. Warwick.
Henry Dennys, son and heir.	= . · · . · · .
John Dennys eldest son and heir, died 1638.	= Margaret, daughter of Sir George Speke, of Whitehackington, co. Somerset.
John Dennys owner of Bitton Farm, died 1660.	= Mary, daughter and co-heir of Nat. Still, of Hutton : died 1698 *annis plena :* buried at Pucklechurch.

No date, it will be perceived, is associated with Sir Walter Dennys, but on referring to a more detailed pedigree from the same source, I find that his eldest son, Sir William Dennys, " founded a guild in the year 1520." We may therefore reasonably assign his birth to the latter part of the fifteenth century, or to the very beginning of the sixteenth. These premises are borne out by the fact that John, his second brother, (author of the " Secrets," according to Sir Harris Nicolas) left a son, Hugh Dennys, who died in 1559, and at no immature age, since he was married and had four offspring. If, therefore, Sir Harris Nicolas's assumption be correct, we must ascribe the poem to the early part, or at the latest, to the middle of the sixteenth century, whereas its style and general character belong, assuredly, to a later period. Collateral evidence, on the side of Mr. Ellacombe's opinion, is to be found in the fact that R. J. (Roger Jackson) in his dedication, does not throw the poem far back, in a posthumous sense, but merely says :—

" This poem being sent unto me to be printed after the death of the author, who intended to have done it, in his life, but was prevented by death," &c. &c.

Had the " Secrets " been in existence half a century, some allusion would surely have been made to the circumstance.

Mr. Carew Hazlitt, in his " Handbook to Early English Literature," cites the bibliography of the book under notice as being "very unsettled."   I had hoped he would have contributed something to its settlement, but he leaves it as he found it. "There seem to have been four editions," he says, "the second and third undated." I have shown that the unique copy of the second is, in all probability, undated, only through the misdoing of the binder's knife, and that of the third, a copy is extant *with* the date. In Mr. Hazlitt's description of the Bodleian côpy of the first edition, he appears to have been guided by Bohn's Lowndes, for he adopts (as I did myself, in the first instance, from want of evidence) one of the blunders of that authority. The copy in question is *not* Milner's copy, which is thus described in his sale-catalogue :—" Denny's *Secrets of Angling,* a Poem, augmented with many approved Experiments by Lauson, *frontispiece, date cut off."* This was evidently, therefore, a mutilated copy of the edition of 1652, in which alone the woodcut figures as a frontispiece. The Bodleian copy, on the contrary, is complete; has no mention of Lauson on the title-page and bears the imprint of 1613. It must have found its way into the library at an earlier date, for two compilers of Angling-book lists, (in MS.) Mr. White of Crickhowell (in 1806-7) and Mr. Appleby (in 1820) refer to it. The former states that it was entered under the name of John Davies, of Kidwelly.

In further corroboration of Mr. Ellacombe's view, I must add that it is adopted by Mr. Tomkins, a descendant of the Dennises of Pucklechurch. (See Notes and Queries. 4th Series, Aug. 28th, 1869.)

The only contemporary recognition of I. D., that I am acquainted with, is in "the Pleasures of Princes, good mens recreations : containing a discourse of the Generall Art of Fishing with the Angle or otherwise ; and of all the hidden Secrets belonging thereunto. Together with the Choyce, Ordering, Breeding, and Dyeting of the Fighting Cocke,"—the latter being added, peradventure, for increase of princeliness. This scarce tract is commonly considered to be the transmigration of the "Secrets" into prose. It first appeared with separate pagination in "The second booke of the English Husbandman," 1614, and in subsequent issues of that work ; and was also incorporated with Markham's "Country Contentments," possibly in 1623, but certainly in 1631 and afterwards. In the latter form it is entitled : "The whole Art of Angling ; as it was written in a small Treatise in Rime, and now, for the better understanding of the Reader, put into Prose and adorned and enlarged." The transmuting process (for there can be little doubt of the correctness of the general surmise) was

effected by no unskilful hand, and without too much sacrifice of the precious
metal of the original.   Sir Philip Sidney's ordeal has, indeed, seldom been
undergone, with so little deterioration.   The quaint character of the poem is
preserved in the prose version and the passages added (especially the introduction)
have a striking merit of their own.

It is proof of the vitality of Dennys' verse, that it retains its strength,
sweetness and savour in its more sober form.   Those curious in parallels may
compare "The Qualities of an Angler," in the third book of the poem, with
chapter 2 (its corresponding passage) of the "Pleasures of Princes."

It is not needful that I should enter on a critical appreciation of this little
poem, the finest passages of which are well known and highly esteemed.   Thus
much, however, may be said, that, so replete is it, in its higher moods, with
subtlety of rhythm, sweetness of expression, and elevation of thought and
feeling, that even from the angling point of view, we cannot but consider it a
notable piece of condescension, and marvel at the devotion of so much real
poetic genius to a theme so humble.   With the exception of the "Compleat
Angler," no higher compliment than this poem has been paid to the sport.
Subsequent rhymers, indeed, have achieved analogous feats, but from other
heights, or rather from other depths—witness the "Innocent Epicure," a polished
piece of artificiality, and often grotesque, by force of polish ; and "The Anglers,
Eight Dialogues in Verse," by Scott of Ipswich, in which the technical and
humorous are dexterously enough interwoven ; but such trifling in verse, as
these and other poems of their kind display, is not to be confounded for an
instant with the art-work and heart-work of John Dennys, (the Angler's "Glorious
John ") who could not have been more in earnest, had he sung of men and
angels ; who drapes himself in his singing robes on the very threshold of his
theme, as by an assured vocation, and only doffs them with his ultimate
line :—

> "And now we are arivèd at the last,
>   In wishèd harbour where we meane to rest ;
> And make an end of this our journey past ;
>   Here then in quiet roade I think it best
> We strike our sailes and stedfast Anchor cast,
>   For now the sunne low setteth in the west."

And " in quiet roade," in the grey old aisle of Pucklechurch, our poet's rest is won :—

> " Such a sleep he sleeps, the man we love ! "

—this man that may have seen the face of Shakespeare, nay, this man that, perchance, fished in his immortal company, the Boyd that he loved and sung so well—the Boyd that still, with " crooked, winding way,"—

> " Its mother Avon runneth soft to seek."

T. WESTWOOD.

ADVERTISEMENT.

THE present reprint is a strictly faithful and literal transcript of the edition of 1613. It has been our wish to perpetuate the original text as the author bequeathed it to the world. In this respect it differs essentially from Mr. Arber's reprint in his "English Garner." Mr. Arber, on the contrary, has thought it expedient to make many changes in the poem, and to introduce into it frequent supposed emendations. Thus he has altered the punctuation throughout and modernised both the orthography and the syntax, robbing the verse, thereby, of much of its ancient air and aspect. Instead of J. D. in his customary doublet and hose, he has given us a J. D. in the broadcloth of to-day, with all the gloss upon it. How far we have a right so to interfere with poets who are no longer here to defend themselves and to protect their own—how far it is justifiable, to submit them to our individual and arbitrary, not to say dogmatic, judgment, is a question we do not take on ourselves to decide. What our own personal opinion in the matter is will be deduced from the course we have adopted.

T. W.

THE

SECRETS OF ANGLING:

Teaching,
The Choisest Tooles Baytes and seasons, for the
taking of any Fish, in Pond or Riuer:
practised and familiarly opened
in three Bookes.

By I. D. *Esquire.*

Worthy Syr,

This Poeme being sent vnto me to be printed after the death of the Author, who intended to haue done it in his life, but was preuented by death: I could not among my good friends, bethinke me of any one to whom I might more fitly dedicate it (as well for the nature of the subiect in which you delight as to expresse my loue) than to yourselfe.

I finde it not onely sauouring of Art and Honesty, two things now strangers vnto many Authors, but also both pleasant and profitable; and being loath to see a thing of such value lye hidden in obscuritie, whilst matters of no moment pester the stales of euery STATIONER; I therefore make holde to publish it, for the benefit and delight of all, trusting that I shall neither thereby disparage the Author, nor dislike them.

I neede not, I think, Appollogize either the vse of the subiect, or for that it is reduced into the nature of a Poeme; for as touching the last (in that it is in verse) some count it by so much the more delightfull; and I holde it euery was as fit a subiect for Poetry as Husbandry: and touching the first, if Hunting and Hawking haue been thought worthy delights and Artes to be instructed in, I make no doubt but this Art of Angling is much more worthy practise and approbation; for it is a sport euery way as pleasant, lesse chargeable, more profitable, and nothing so much subiect to choller or impatience as those are: you shall finde it more briefly, pleasantly, and exactly performed, then any of this kinde heretofore. Therefore I referre you to the perusing thereof, and myselfe to your good opinion, which I tender as that I holde most deere: euer remaining at

Your gentle Command,

R. I.

IN DUE PRAISE OF THIS PRAISE-WORTHY
SKILL AND *WORKE.*

I N *skils* that *all* doe seeke, but *few* doe *finde*,
    Both *gaine* and *game ;* (like *Sunne* and *Moone* doe shine)
    Then th' *Art* of *Fishing* thus, is of that kinde ;
    The Angler taketh both with *Hooke* and *Line,*
And as, with *Lines,* both these he takes; this takes,
With many a *Line,* well made, both *Eares* and *Harts ;*
And, by this *skill,* the skill-lesse skill-full makes :
The *Corpes* whereof dissected so he parts,
Vpon an humble *Subiect* neuer lay,
More proude, yet plainer *Lines,* the *plaine* to leade,
This playner *Art* with *pleasure* to suruay,
To purchase it, with *profit,* by that *DEED :*
    Who thinke this *skill's* too *low* than, for the *high,*
    This *Angler* reade, and they'l be *tane* thereby.

Io. DAUIES.

THE CONTENTS.

THE FIRST BOOKE CONTAINETH THESE 3. HEADS.

THE SECOND BOOKE, CONTAINETH

THE THIRD BOOKE CONTAINETH,

D

THE

SECRETS

of ANGLING.

———◆———

THE FIRST BOOKE.

F *Angling*, and the Art thereof I sing,
What kinde of Tooles it doth behoue to haue;
And with what pleasing bayt a man may bring
The Fish to bite within the watry waue.
    A worke of thankes to such as in a thing
Of harmlesse pleasure, haue regard to saue
      Their dearest soules from sinne; and may intend
      Of pretious time, some part thereon to spend.

You *Nymphs* that in the Springs and Waters sweet,
Your dwelling haue, of euery Hill and Dale,
And oft amidst the Meadows greene doe meet
To sport and play, and heare the *Nightingale;*
And in the Riuers fresh doe wash your feet,
While *Prognes* sister tels her wofull tale:
      Such ayde and power vnto my verses lend,
      As may suffice this little worke to end.

And thou sweet *Boyd*[1] that with thy watry sway,
 Dost wash the cliffes of *Deington* and of *Weeke;*
And through their Rockes with crooked winding way,
Thy mother *Auon* runnest soft to seeke :
In whose fayre streames the speckled *Trout* doth play,
The *Roche,* the *Dace,* the *Gudgin,* and the *Bleeke.*

      Teach me the skill with slender Line and Hooke
      To take each Fish of Riuer, Pond, and Brooke.

THE TIME FOR PROUIDING ANGLE RODS.

First, when the Sunne beginneth to decline
Southward his course, with his fayre Chariot bright,
And passed hath of Heauen the middle Line,
That makes of equall length both day and night ;
And left behind his backe the dreadfull signe,
Of cruell *Centaure,* slaine in drunken fight,

      When Beasts do mourne, and Birds forsake their song,
      And euery Creature thinkes the night too long.

And blustring *Boreas* with his chilling cold,
Vnclothed hath the Trees of Sommers greene ;
And Woods, and groues, are naked to behold,
Of Leaues and Branches now dispoyled cleane :
So that their fruitfull stocks they doe vnfold,
And lay abroad their of-spring to be seene ;

      Where nature shewes her great increase of kinde
      To such as seeke their tender shutes to finde.

Then goe into some great *Arcadian* wood,
Where store of ancient *Hazels* doe abound ;
And seeke amongst their springs and tender brood ;
Such shutes as are the straightest, long, and round :
And of them all (store vp what you thinke good)
But fairest choose, the smoothest, and most sound ;

      So that they doe not two yeares growth exceed.
      In shape and beautie like the *Belgicke* Reed.

[1] The name of a Brooke.

These prune and clense of euery leafe and spray,
Yet leaue the tender top remaining still:
Then home with thee goe beare them safe away,
But perish not the Rine and vtter Pill;
And on some euen boarded floore them lay,
Where they may dry and season at their fill:
     And place vpon their crooked parts some waight,
      To presse them downe, and keepe them plaine and straight.

So shalt thou haue alwayes in store the best,
And fittest Rods to serue thy turne aright;
For not the brittle *Cane*, nor all the rest,
I like so well, though it be long and light,
Since that the Fish are frighted with the least
Aspect of any glittering thing, or white:
     Nor doth it by one halfe so well incline,
      As doth the plyant rod to saue the line.

TO MAKE THE LINE.

Then get good Hayre, so that it be not blacke,
Neither of Mare nor Gelding let it be;
Nor of the tyreling Iade that beares the packe:
But of some lusty Horse or Courser free,
Whose bushie tayle, vpon the ground doth tracke,
Like blazing *Comete* that sometimes we see:
     From out the mid'st thereof the longest take,
      At leysure best your Linkes and Lines to make.

Then twist them finely, as you thinke most meet,
By skill or practise easie to be found;
As doth *Arachne* with her slender feet;
Draw forth her little thread along the ground:
But not too hard or slacke, the meane is sweet,
Least slacke they snarle, or hard they proue vnsound,
     And intermixt with siluer, silke, or gold,
      The tender hayres, the better so to hold.

Then end to end, as falleth to their lot,
Let all your Linkes in order as they lie
Be knit together, with that Fishers knot
That will not slip, nor with the wet vntie:
And at the lowest end forget it not
To leaue a Bought or Compasse like an eye,
     The Linke that holds your Hooke to hang vpon,
     When you thinke good to take it off and on.

Which Linke must neither be so great nor strong,
Nor like of colour as the others were;
Scant halfe so big, so that it be as long:
Of greyest Hue, and of the soundest Hayre,
Least whiles it hangs the liquid waues among
The sight thereof, the warie Fish should feare.
     And at one end a Loope or Compasse fine,
     To fasten to the other of your line.

CORKE.

Then take good *Corke*, as much as shall suffice,
For euery Line to make his swimmer fit;
And where the midst and thickest parts doth rise,
There burne a round small hole quite thorow it:
And put therein a Quill of equall size,
But take good heed the *Corke* you do not slit.
     Then round or square with *Rasor* pare it neare,
     Piramid-wise, or like a slender Peare.

The smaller end doth serue to sinke more light,
Into the water with the Plummets sway:
The greater swims aloft and stands vpright,
To keepe the Line and Bayt at euen stay,
That when the Fish begins to nib and byte,
The mouing of the float doth them bewray:
     These may you place upon your Lines at will,
     And stoppe them with a white and handsome Quill.

HOOKES.

Then buy your Hookes the finest and the best
That may be had of such as vse to sell,
And from the greatest to the very least
Of euery sort picke out and chuse them well,
Such as in shape and making passe the rest,
And doe for strength and soundnesse most excell :
      Then in a little Boxe of dryest wood
        From rust and canker keepe them faire and good.

That Hooke I loue that is in compasse round,
Like to the print that *Pegasus* did make,
With horned hoofe vpon *Thessalian* ground ;
From whence forthwith *Pernassus* spring out brake,
That doth in pleasant Waters so abound :
And of the *Muses* oft the thirst doth slake ;
      Who on his fruitfull bankes doe sit and sing,
        That all the world of their swee[t] tunes doth ring.

Or as *Thaumantis*, when she list to shrowd
Herselfe against the parching sunny ray,
Vnder the mantle of some stormy cloud,
Where she her sundry colours doth display
Like *Iunoes* bird, of her faire garments proud,
That *Phœbus* gaue her on her marriage day :
      Shewes forth her goodly Circle farre and wide
        To mortall wights that wonder at her pride.

His *Shank* should neither be too short nor long,
His point not ouersharpe, nor yet too dull :
The substance good that may indure from wrong ;
His Needle slender, yet both round and full,
Made of the right *Iberian* mettell strong,
That will not stretch nor breake at euery pull,
      Wrought smooth and cleane withouten crack or knot
        And bearded like the wilde *Arabian* goat.

Then let your Hooke be sure and strongly plaste
Vnto your lowest Linke with Silke or Hayre,
Which you may doe with often ouercaste,
So that you draw the Bouts together neare,
And with both ends make all the other fast,
That no bare place or rising knot appeare :
  Then on that Linke hang Leads of euen waight
  To raise your floate, and carry down your baite.

Thus have you *Rod, Line, Float* and *Hooke ;*
The Rod to strike, when you shall thinke it fit,
The Line to lead the Fish with wary skill,
The Float and Quill to warne you of the bit ;
The Hooke to hold him by the chap or gill,
Hooke, Line, and Rod, all guided to your wit.
  Yet there remaines of Fishing tooles to tell,
  Some other sorts that you must haue as well.

OTHER FISHING TOOLES.

A little Boord, the lightest you can finde,
But not so thin that it will breake or bend ;
Of *Cypres* sweet, or of some other kinde,
That like a Trenchor shall itselfe extend :
Made smooth and plaine, your Lines thereon to winde,
With Battlements at euery other end :
  Like to the Bulwarke of some ancient Towne
  As well-wald Sylchester now razed downe.

A Shooe to beare the crawling Wormes therein, ·
With hole aboue to hang it by your side,
A hollow Cane that must be light and thin,
Wherein the *Bobb* and *Palmer* shall abide,
Which must be stopped with an handsome pin,
Least out againe your baytes doe hap to slide.
  A little Box that couered close shall lye,
  To keepe therein the busie winged Flye.

Then must you haue a Plummet, formed round,
Like to the Pellet of a birding Bow:
Wherewith you may the secret'st waters sound,
And set your floate thereafter high, or low,
Till you the depth thereof haue truly found:
And on the same a twisted thread bestow
    At your owne will, to hang it on your hooke,
    And so to let it downe into the Brooke.

Of Lead likewise, yet must you haue a Ring,
Whose whole Diameter in length containes
Three Inches full, and fastned to a string
That must be long and sure, if need constraines:
Through whose round hole you shall your Angle bring,
And let it fall into the watry playne:
    Vntill he come the weedes and stickes vnto,
    From whence your hooke it serueth to vndo.

Haue Tooles good store to serue your turne withall,
Least that you happen some to lose or breake;
As in great waters oft it doth befall,
When that the Hooke is nought or Line too weake.
And waxed thread, or silke, so it be small,
To set them on, that if you list to wreake
    Your former losse, you may supply the place,
    And not returne with sorrow and disgrace.

Haue twist likewise, so that it be not white,
You Rod to mend, or broken top to tye;
For all white colours doe the Fishes fright
And make them from the bayte away to flye;
A File to mend your hookes, both small and light,
A good sharpe knife, your Girdle hanging by:
    A Pouch with many parts and purses thin,
    To carry all your Tooles and Trynkets in.

E

Yet must you haue a little Rip beside
Of Willow twigs, the finest you can wish ;
Which shall be made so handsome and so wide
As may containe good store of sundry Fish :
And yet with ease be hanged by your side,
To bring them home the better to your dish.
    A little Net that on a Pole shall stand,
    The mighty Pike or heauy Carpe to Land.

HIS SEUERALL TOOLES, AND WHAT GARMENT IS FITTEST.

And let your garments Russet be or gray,
Of colour darke, and hardest to descry :
That with the Raine or weather will away,
And least offend the fearefull Fishes eye :
For neither Skarlet nor rich cloth of ray
Nor colours dipt in fresh *Assyrian* dye,
    Nor tender silkes, of Purple, Paule, or golde,
    Will scrue so well to keepe off wet or cold.

In this aray the *Angler* good shall goe
Vnto the Brooke, to finde his wished game ;
Like old *Menalcus* wandring to and fro,
Vntil he chance to light vpon the same,
And there his art and cunning shall bestow,
For euery Fish his bayte so well to frame,
    That long ere *Phœbus* set in Westerne fome,
    He shall returne well loaden to his home.

OBIECTION.

Some youthfull *Gallant* here perhaps will say
This is no pastime for a gentleman.
It were more fit at cardes and dice to play,
To use both fence and dauncing now and than,
Or walke the streetes in nice and strange Aray,
Or with coy phrases court his Mistris fan,
    A poore delight with toyle and painfull watch,
    With losse of time a silly Fish to catch.

The Secrets of Angling.

What pleasure can it be to walke about,
The fields and meades in heat or pinching cold?
And stand all day to catch a silly *Trout*,
That is not worth a teaster to be sold,
And peraduenture sometimes goe without,
Besides the toles and troubles manifold,
     And to be washt with many a showre of rayne,
     Before he can returne from thence again?

More ease it were, and more delight I trow,
In some sweet house to passe the time away,
Amongst the best, with braue and gallant show,
And with faire dames to daunce, to sport and play,
And on the board, the nimble dice to throw,
That brings in gaine, and helps the shot to pay,
     And with good wine and store of dainty fare,
     To feede at will and take but little care.

THE ANSWERE.

I meane not here mens errours to reproue,
Nor do enuie their seeming happy state;
But rather meruaile why they doe not loue
An honest sport that is without debate;
Since their abused pastimes often moue
Their mindes to anger and to mortall hate:
     And as in bad delights their time they spend,
     So oft it brings them to no better end.

Indeed it is a life of lesser paine,
To sit at play from noone till it be night:
And then from night till it be noone againe,
With damned oathes, pronounced in despight,
For little cause and euery trifle vaine,
To curse, to brawle, to quarrell, and to fight,
     To packe the Cardes, and with some cozning tricke,
     His fellowes Purse of all his coyne to picke.

Or to beguile auother of his Wife,
As did *Æghistus Agamemnon* serue :
Or as that Roman [1] monarch led a life
To spoil and spend, while others pine and sterue,
And to compell their friends with foolish strife,
To take more drinke then will their health preserue :
　　　　And to conclude, for debt or iust desart,
　　　　In baser tune to sing the *Counter*-part.

O let me rather on the pleasant Brinke
Of *Tyne* and *Trent* possesse some dwelling-place ;
Where I may see my Quill and Corke downe sinke,
With eager bit of *Barbill*, *Bleike*, or *Dace :*
And on the World and his Creator thinke,
While they proud *Thais* painted sheat imbrace.
　　　　And with the fume of strong *Tobacco's* smoke,
　　　　All quaffing round are ready for to choke.

Let them that list these pastimes then pursue,
And on their pleasing fancies feede their fill ;
So I the Fields and Meadowes greene may view,
And by the Riuers fresh may walke at will,
Among the *Dayzes* and the *Violets* blew :
Red *Hyacinth* and yealow *Daffadill*,
　　　　Purple *Narcissus*, like the morning rayes,
　　　　Pale *Ganderglas* and azour *Culuerkayes.*

I count it better pleasure to behold
The goodly compasse of the loftie Skye,
And in the midst thereof like burning gold
The flaming Chariot of the worlds great eye ;
The watry cloudes that in the ayre vprold
With sundry kindes of painted collours flie : ·
　　　　And fayre *Aurora* lifting vp her head,
　　　　And blushing rise from old *Thitonus* bed.

[1] Nero.

The hills and Mountaines raised from the Plaines,
The plaines extended leuell with the ground,
The ground deuided into sundry vaines,
The vaines inclos'd with running riuers rounde,
The riuers making way through natures chaine,
With headlong course into the sea profounde:
    The surging sea beneath the valleys low,
    The valleys sweet, and lakes that lonely flowe.

The lofty woods the forrests wide and long,
Adornd with leaues and branches fresh and greene,
In whose coole bow'rs the birds with chaunting song,
Doe welcome with thin quire the *Summers* Queene,
The meadowes faire where *Flora's* guifts among,
Are intermixt the verdant grasse betweene,
    The siluer skaled fish that softlie swimme,
    Within the brookes and Cristall watry brimme.

All these and many more of his creation,
That made the heauens, the *Angler* oft doth see,
And takes therein no little delectation,
To think how strange and wonderfull they be,
Framing thereof an inward contemplation,
To set his thoughts from other fancies free,
    And whiles hee lookes on these with ioyfull eye,
    His minde is rapt aboue the starry skye.

THE AUTHOR OF ANGLING.

Bvt how this Art of Angling did beginne,
And who the vse thereof and practise found,
How many times and ages since haue bin,
Wherein the sunne hath dayly compast round,
The circle that the signes twice sixe are in :
And yeelded yearely comfort to the ground,
    It were too hard for me to bring about,
    Since *Ouid* wrote not all that story out.

Yet to content the willing Readers eare,
I will not spare the sad report to tell,
When good *Deucalion* and his *Pirrha* deere,
Were onely left vpon the earth to dwell
Of all the rest that ouerwhelmed were
With that great floud, that in their dayes befell,
  Wherein the compasse of the world so round,
  Both man and beast with waters deepe were dround.

Between themselues they wept and made great moane,
How to repaire againe the wofull fall,
Of all mankinde, whereof they two alone
The remnant were, and wretched portion small,
But any meanes or hope in them was none,
That might restore so great a losse with all,
  Since they were aged, and in yeares so runne,
  That now almost their threed of life was spunne.

Vntill at last they saw where as there stood
An ancient Temple, wasted and forlorne ;
Whose holy fires and sundry offerings good,
The late outragious waues away had borne :
But when at length downe fallen was the flood,
The waters low it proudly gan to scorne.
  Vnto that place they thought it best to goe,
  The counsell of the *Goddesse* there to know.

For long before that fearfull *Deluge* great,
The vniuersall Earth had ouerflowne ;
A heauenly power there placed had her seate,
And answeres gaue of hidden things vnknowne.
Thither they went her fauour to intreat,
Whose fame throughout that coast abroad was blowne.
  By her aduice some way or meane to finde,
  How to renew the race of humane kind.

Prostrate they fell vpon the sacred ground,
Kissing the stones, and shedding many a teare ;
And lowly bent their aged bodies downe
Vnto the earth, with sad and heauy cheare ;
Praying the Saint with soft and dolefull sound
That she vouchsafe their humble suite to heare.
      The *Goddesse* heard, and bad them goe and take,
      Their mothers bones, & throw behind their backe.

This *Oracle* obscure, and darke of sence,
Amazed much their mindes with feare and doubt,
What kind of meaning might be drawne from thence ;
And how to vnderstand and finde it out,
How with so great a sinne they might dispense
Their Parents bones to cast and throw about :
      Thus when they had long time in studie spent,
      Out of the Church with carefull thought they went.

And now beholding better euery place,
Each Hill and Dale, each Riuer, Rock, and Tree ;
And muzing thereupon a little space,
They thought the Earth their mother well might be,
And that the stones that lay before their face,
To be her bones did nothing disagree :
      Wherefore to proue if it were false or true,
      The scattered stones behind their backs they threw.

Forthwith the stones (a wondrous thing to heare)
Began to moue as they had life conceiu'd,
And waxed greater than at first they were ;
And more and more the shape of man receiu'd,
Till euery part most plainely did appeare,
That neither eye nor sence could be deceiu'd :
      They heard, they spake, they went, and walked too,
      As other liuing men are wont to doe.

Thus was the earth replenished a new
With people strange, sprung vp with little paine,
Of whose increase the progenie that grew,
Did soone supply the empty world againe ;
But now a greater care there did insue,
How such a mightie number to maintaine,
     Since foode there was not any to be found,
      For that great flood had all destroyd and drownd.

Then did *Deucalion* first the Art inuent
Of *Angling*, and his people taught the same ;
And to the Woods and groues with them hee went
Fit tooles to finde for this most needfull game ;
There from the trees the longest ryndes they rent,
Wherewith strong Lines they roughly twist and frame,
     And of each crooke of hardest Bush and Brake,
      They made them Hookes the hungry Fish to take.

And to intice them to the eager bit,
Dead frogs and flies of sundry sorts he tooke ;
And snayles and wormes such as he found most fit,
Wherein to hide the close and deadly hooke :
And thus with practise and inuentiue wit,
He found the meanes in euery lake and brooke
     Such store of Fish to take with little paine,
      As did long time this people new sustaine.

In this rude sorte began this simple Art,
And so remain'd in that first age of old,
When *Saturne* did *Amaltheas* horne impart
Vnto the world, that then was all of Gold ;
The Fish as yet had felt but little smart,
And were to bite more eager, apt, and bold :
     And plentie still supplide the place againe
      Of woefull want, whereof we now complaine.

But when in time the feare and dread of man
Fell more and more on every liuing thing,
And all the creatures of the world began
To stand in awe of this vsurping King,
Whose tyranny so farre extended than
That Earth and Seas it did in thraldome bring ;
    It was a worke of greater paine and skill,
    The wary Fish in lake or Brooke to kill.

So worse and worse two ages more did passe,
Yet still this Art more perfect daily grew,
For then the slender Rod inuented was,
Of finer sort than former ages knew,
And Hookes were made of siluer and of brasse,
And Lines of Hempe and Flaxe were framed new,
    And sundry baites experience found out more,
    Then elder times did know or try before.

But at the last the Iron age drew neere,
Of all the rest the hardest, and most scant,
Then Lines were made of Silke and subtile hayre
And Rods of lightest Cane and Hazell plant,
And Hookes of hardest steele inuented were,
That neither skill nor workemanship did want,
    And so this Art did in the end attaine
    Vnto that state where now it doth remaine.

But here my weary *Muse* a while must rest,
That is not vsed to so long a way ;
And breath, or pause a little at the least
At this Lands end, vntill another day,
And then againe, if so she thinke it best :
Our taken-taske afresh wee will assay,
    And forward goe as first we did intend,
    Till that wee come vnto our iourneyes end.

        The end of the first Book.

THE SECOND BOOKE.

EFORE, I taught what kinde of Tooles were fit
For him to haue that would an *Angler* be:
And how he should with practise and with wit
Prouide himselfe thereof in best degree:
Now doth remaine to shew how to the bit
The Fishes may be brought, that earst were free,
And with what pleasing baits intis'd they are,
To swallow downe the hidden Hooke vnware.

BAITES.

It were not meet to send a Huntsman out
Into the Woods, with Net, with Gin, or Hay,
To trace the brakes and bushes all about,
The *Stag*, the *Foxe*, or *Badger* to betray:
It hauing found his game, he stand in doubt
Which way to pitch, or where his snares to lay,
And with what traine he may entise withall
The fearfull beast into his trap to fall.

So, though the *Angler* haue good store of tooles,
And them with skill in finest sort can frame;
Yet when he comes to Riuers, Lakes, and Pooles,
If that he know not how to vse the same,
And with what baits to make the Fishes fooles,
He may goe home as wise as out he came,
And of his comming boast himselfe as well
As he that from his fathers Chariot fell.

Not that I take vpon mee to impart
More then by others hath before beene told ;
Or that the hidden secrets of this Art
I would vnto the vulgar sort vnfolde,
Who peraduenture for my paines desart
Would count me worthy *Balams* horse to holde :
      But onely to the willing learner show
      So much thereof as may suffise to know.

But here, O *Neptune*, that with triple Mace
Dost rule the raging of the *Ocean* wide ;
I meddle not with thy deformed race
Of monsters huge, that in those waues abide :
With that great Whale, that by three whole dayes space
The man of God did in his belly hide,
      And cast him out vpon the *Euxin* shore
      As safe and sound as he had beene before.

Nor with that *Orke* that on *Cephæan* strand
Would haue deuour'd *Andremeda* the faire,
Whom *Perseus* slew with strong and valiant hand,
Deliuering her from danger and despaire,
The *Hurlepoole* huge that higher then the land,
Whole streames of water spouteth in the ayre,
      The *Porpois* large that playing swims on hie,
      Portending stormes or other tempest nie.

Nor that admirer of sweet Musickes sound,
That on his backe *Arion* bore away ;
And brought to shore out of the Seas profound,
The *Hippotame* that like an horse doth neigh,
The *Mors*, that from the rockes inrolled round,
Within his teeth himselfe doth safe conuay :
      The *Tortoise* couered with his target hard,
      The *Tuberone* attended with his guard.

Nor with that Fish that beareth in his snout
A ragged sword, his foes to spoile and kill;
Nor that fierce *Thrasher*, that doth fling about
His nimble flayle, and handles him at will :
The rauenous *Sharke* that with the sweepings out
And filth of ships doth oft his belly fill;
  The *Albacore* that followeth night and day
  The flying Fish, and takes them for his pray.

The *Crocodile* that weepes when he doth wrong,
The *Hollibut* that hurts the appetite,
The *Turbut* broad, the *Sceale*, the *Sturgion* strong.
The *Cod* and *Cozze*, that greedy are to bite,
The *Haake*, the *Haddocke*, and *Conger* long,
The yeallow *Ling*, the *Milwell* faire and white,
  The spreading *Ray*, the *Thornback* thin and flat,
  The boysterous *Base*, the hoggish *Tunny* fat.

These kindes of Fish that are so large of sise,
And many more that here I leaue vntolde
Shall goe for me, and all the rest likewise
That are the flocke of *Proteus* watry folde :
For well I thinke my Hookes wovld not suffise,
Nor slender Lines, the least of these to holde.
  I leaue them therefore to the surging Seas :
  In that huge depth, to wander at their ease.

And speake of such as in the fresh are found,
The little *Roach*, the *Menise* biting fast,
The slymie *Tench*, the slender *Smelt* and round,
The *Umber* sweet, the *Graueling* good of taste,
The wholesome *Ruffe*, the *Barbill* not so sound,
The *Pearch* and *Pike* that all the rest doe waste,
  The *Bream*, the *Carpe*, the *Chub*, and *Chauendar*,
  And many more that in fresh waters are.

Sit then *Thalia* on some pleasant banke,
Among so many as fair Auon hath,
And marke the *Anglers* how they march in ranke,
Some out of *Bristoll*, some from healthfull *Bath;*
How all the *Riuers* sides along they flanke,
And through the Meadowes make their wonted path :
  See how their wit and cunning they apply,
  To catch the Fish that in the waters lye.

FOR THE GOODGION.

Loe, in a little Boate where one doth stand,
That to a Willow Bough the while is tide,
And with a pole doth stirre and raise the sand ;
Where as the gentle streame doth softly glide,
And then with slender Line and Rod in hand,
The eager bit not long he doth abide.
  Well leaded is his Line, his Hooke but small,
  A good big Corke to beare the streame withall.

His baite the least red worme that may be found,
And at the bottome it doth alwayes lye ;
Whereat the greedy *Goodgion* bites so sound
That Hooke and all he swalloweth by and by :
See how he strikes, and puls them vp as round
As if new store the play did still supply.
  And when the bit doth dye or bad doth proue,
  Then to another place he doth remoue.

This Fish the fittest for a learner is
That in that Art delights to take some paine ;
For as high flying Haukes that often misse
The swifter foules, are eased with a traine,
So to a young beginner yeeldeth this,
Such readie sport as makes him proue againe,
  And leades him on with hope and glad desire,
  To greater skill, and cunning to aspire.

FOR THE ROCHE

Then see on yonder side, where one doth sit
With Line well twisted, and his Hooke but small;
His Corke not big, his Plummets round and fit,
His bayt of finest paste, a little ball
Wherewith he doth intice vnto the bit,
The careless *Roche*, that soone is caught withall:
> Within a foote the same doth reach the ground.
> And with least touch the float straight sinketh downe.

And as a skilfull Fowler that doth vse
The flying Birds of any kinde to take,
The fittest and the best doth alwayes chuse,
Of many sorts a pleasing stale to make,
Which if he doth perceiue they doe refuse,
And of mislike abandon and forsake,
> To win their loue againe, and get their grace
> Forthwith doth put another in the place.

So for the Roach more baites he hath beside,
As of a sheepe the thicke congealed blood,
Which on a board he vseth to deuide
In portions small, to make them fit and good,
That better on his hooke they may abide:
And of the waspe the white and tender brood,
> And wormes that breed on euery hearbe and tree,
> And sundry flies that quicke and liuely be.

FOR THE DACE.

Then looke where as that Poplar gray doth grow,
Hard by the same where one doth closely stand,
And with the winde his Hooke and bayt doth throw
Amid the streame with slender hazell wand,
Where as he sees the *Dace* themselues doe show,
His eye is quicke, and ready is his hand,
> And when the Fish doth rise to catch the bayt,
> He presently doth strike, and takes her strayt.

O worlds deceit! how are we thrald by thee,
Thou dost thy gall in sweetest pleasures hide?
When most we thinke in happiest state to be,
Then doe we soonest into danger slide,
Behold the Fish that euen now was free,
Vnto the deadly hooke how he is tide,
      So vaine delights alure vs to the snare,
      Wherein vnwares we fast intangled are.

FOR THE CARPE.

Bvt now againe see where another stands,
And straines his rod that double seemes to bend,
Loe how he leades and guides him with his hands,
Least that his line should breake or Angle rend,
Then with a Net see how at last he lands,
A mighty *Carpe* and has him in the end,
      So large he is of body, scale, and bone,
      That rod and all had like to haue beene gone.

Marke what a line he hath, well made and strong,
Of *Bucephall*, or *Bayards* strongest hayre,
Twisted with greene or watched silke among,
Like hardest twine, that holds th' intangled Deare,
Not any force of Fish will doe it wrong,
In *Tyne*, or *Trent*, or *Thame* he needes not feare:
      The knots of euery lincke are knit so sure,
      That many a plucke and pull they may indure.

His corke is large, made handsome, smooth, and fine,
The leads according, close and fit, thereto,
A good round hooke set on with silken twine,
That will not slip nor easily vndoe:
His bait great wormes that long in mosse haue bin,
Which by his side he beareth in a shooe.
      Or paste wherewith he feedes him oft before,
      That at the bottom lyes a foote or more.

FOR THE CHUB AND TROUT.

See where another hides himselfe as slye,
As did *Acteon*, or the fearefull Deere ;
Behinde a withy, and with watchfull eye
Attends the bit within the water cleere,
And on the top thereof doth moue his flye,
With skilfull hand, as if he liuing were.
>   Loe how the *Chub*, the *Roche*, the *Dace*, and *Trout*,
>   To catch thereat doe gaze and swimme about.

His Rod, or Cane, made darke for being seene,
The lesse to feare the warie Fish withall :
The Line well twisted is, and wrought so cleane
That being strong, yet doth it shew but small,
His Hooke not great, nor little, but betweene,
That light vpon the watry brimme may fall,
>   The Line in length scant halfe the Rod exceedes,
>   And neither Corke, nor Leade thereon it needes.

FOR THE TROUT, AND EELE.

Now see some standing where the streame doth fall,
With headlong course behind the sturdy weere,
That ouerthwart the riuer, like a wall,
The water stops, and strongly vp doth beare,
And at the Tayles, of Mills and Arches small,
Where as the shoote is swift and not too cleare,
>   Their lines in length not twice aboue an ell,
>   But with good store of lead and twisted well.

Round handsome hookes that will not breake nor bend,
The big red worm, well scowred, is their bayte,
Which downe vnto the bottome doth discend.
Whereas the *Trout* and *Eele* doth lye in wayte,
And to their feeding busily intend,
Which when they see they snatch and swallow straight.
>   Vpon their lines are neither Corke nor Quill,
>   But when they feele them plucke then strike they stil.

FOR THE SEWANT AND FLOUNDER.

Behold some others ranged all along,
To take the *Sewant*, yea, the *Flounder* sweet,
That to the banke in deepest places throng,
To shunne the swifter streame that runnes so fleete,
And lye and feede the brackish waues among,
Whereas the waters fresh and salt doe meete:
      And there the *Eele* and *Shad* sometimes is caught,
      That with the tide into the brookes are brought.

.

But by the way it shall not be amisse,
To vnderstand that in the waters gray,
Of floating Fish, two sundry kindes there is,
The one that liues by rauen and by pray,
And of the weaker sort, now that, now this,
He bites, and spoyles, and kills, and beares away,
      And in his greedy gullet doth deuowre,
      As *Scillas* gulfe, a ship within his powre.

And these haue wider mouthes to catch and take
Their flying pray, whom swiftly they pursew,
And rows of teeth like to a saw or rake,
Wherewith the gotten game they bite and chew,
And greater speede within the waters make,
To set vpon the other simple crew,
      And as the grayhound steales vpon the hare,
      So doe they vse to rush on them vnware.

Vnequall Fate, that some are borne to be
Fearfull and milde, and for the rest a pray,
And others are ordain'd to liue more free,
Without controule or danger any way:
So doth the Foxe the Lambe destroy we see,
The *Lyon* fierce, the *Beuer*, *Roe*, or *Gray*,
      The *Hauke*, the foule, the greater wrong the lesse,
      The lofty proud, the lowly poore oppresse.

G

FOR THE PIKE OR PEARCH.

Now for to take these kinde of Fish with all,
It shal be needfull to haue still in store,
Some liuing baites as *Bleiks*, and *Roches* small,
Goodgion, or *Loach*, not taken long before,
Or yealow *Frogges* that in the waters craule,
But all aliue they must be euermore :
      For as for baites that dead and dull doe lye,
      They least esteeme and set but little by.

But take good heed your line be sure and strong,
The knots well knit, and of the soundest hayre,
Twisted with some well coloured silke among,
And that you haue no neede your Rod to feare :
For these great Fish will striue and struggle long,
Rod, line, and all into the streame to beare.
      And that your hooke be not too small and weake,
      Least that it chance to stretch, or hap to breake.

And as in *Arden* or the mountaines hoare,
Of *Appemmie* [Apennine] or craggy *Alps* among,
The mastifes fierce that hunt the bristled Boare,
Are harnesed with *Curats* light and stronge,
So for these Fish, your line a foote or more,
Must armed be with thinnest plate along,
      Or slender wyre well fastned thereunto,
      That will not slip nor easily vndoe.

The other kinde that are vnlike to these
Doe liue by corne or any other seede :
Sometimes by crummes of bread, of paste or cheese,
Or grassehoppers that in greene meadows breed,
With brood of waspes, of hornets, doares or bees,
Lip berries from the bryar bush or weede,
      Bloud wormes, and snayles, or crauling Ientiles small,
      And buzzing flies that on the waters fall.

All these are good, and many others more,
To make fit baites to take these kinde of Fish,
So that some faire deepe place you feede before,
A day or two, with paile, with bole, or dish ;
And of these meats do vse to throw in store,
Then shall you haue them byte as you would wish:
      And ready sport to take your pleasure still,
      Of any sort that best you like to kill.

Thus seruing them as often as you may,
But once a weeke at least it must be done,
If that to bite they make too long delay,
As by your sport may be perceiued soone :
Then some great Fish doth feare the rest away,
Whose fellowship and companie they shunne :
      Who neither in the bait doth take delight,
      Nor yet will suffer them that would to byte.

For this you must a remedie prouide,
Some *Roche* or *Bleike*, as I have shew'd before,
Beneath whose vpper fin you close shall hide
Of all your Hooke the better halfe and more,
And though the point appeare or may be spide,
It makes no matter any whit therefore :
      But let him fall into the watry brimme,
      And downe vnto the bottome softly swimme.

And when you see your Corke begin to moue,
And round about to soare and fetch a ring,
Sometime to sinke, and sometime swimme aboue,
As doth the Ducke within the watry spring,
Yet make no haste your present hap to proue,
Till with your float at last away hee fling,
      Then may you safely strike and hold him short,
      And at your will prolong or end your sport.

But euery Fish loues not each bayte alike,
Although sometime they feede vpon the same ;
But some doe one, and some another seeke,
As best vnto their appetite doth frame,
The *Roche*, the *Bream*, the *Carpe*, the *Chub*, and *Bleik*,
With paste or Corne their greedy hunger tame,
  The *Dace*, the *Ruffe*, the *Goodgion* and the rest,
  The smaller sort of crawling wormes loue best.

The *Chauender* and *Chub* doe more delight
To feede on tender Cheese, or Cherries red,
Blacke snayles, their bellies slit to shew their white,
Or Grashoppers that skip in euery Meade ;
The *Pearch*, the *Tench*, and *Eele*, doe rather bite
At great red wormes, in Field or Garden bred,
  That haue beene scowr'd in mosse or Fenell rough,
  To rid their filth, and make them hard and tough.

And with this bayte hath often taken bin
The *Salmon* faire, of Riuer-fish the best ;
The *Shad*, that in the Spring time commeth in,
The *Suant* swift, that is not set by least,
The *Bocher* sweet, the pleasant *Flounder* thin,
The *Peele*, the *Tweat*, the *Botling*, and the rest,
  With many more, that in the deepe doth lye
  Of *Auon*, *Vske*, of *Seuerne* and of *Wye*.

Alike they bite, alike they pull downe low
The sinking Corke that striues to rise againe,
And when they feele the sudden deadly blow,
Alike they shunne the danger and the paine ;
And as an arrow from the *Scithian* bow,
All flee alike into the streame amaine,
  Vntill the *Angler* by his wary skill,
  There tyres them out, and brings them vp at will.

The Secrets of Angling.

Yet furthermore it doth behoue to know,
That for the most part Fish doe seeke their foode
Vpon the ground, or deepest bottome low,
Or at the top of water, streame, or flood;
And so you must your hooke and bayte bestow,
For in the midst you shall doe little good,
> For heauie things downe to the bottom fall,
> And light doe swim, and seldome sinke at all.

All Summer long aloft the Fishes swimme,
Delighted with faire *Phœbus* shining ray,
And lye in wayte within the waters dimme
For flyes and gnats that on the top doe play;
Then halfe a yard beneath the vpper brimme
It shall be best your bayted Hooke to lay,
> With gnat or fly of any sort or kinde,
> That euery Moneth on Leaues or Trees you finde.

But then your Line must haue no Lead at all,
And but a slender Corke, or little Quill,
To stay the bayte that downe it doe not fall,
But hang a Linke within the water still,
Or else vpon the top thereof you shall
With quicker hand, and with more ready skill
> Let fall your flye, and now and then remoue,
> Which soone the Fish will finde and better loue.

And in the streame likewise they vse to be
At tailes of floudyates, or at Arches wide;
Or shallow flats, whereas the waters free
With fresher springs and swifter course doe slide:
And then of Waspe, the brood that cannot flye
Vpon a Tyle-stone first a little dryed,
> Or yealow bobs turned vp before the Plough,
> Are chiefest bayts, with Corke and Lead enough.

But when the golden Chariot of the Sunne,
Departing from our Northern countries farre
Beyond the ballance, now his course hath runne
And goes to warme the cold *Antarticque* starre,
And Summers heat is almost spent and done,
With new approach of Winters dreadfull warre :
  Then doe the Fish withdraw into the deepe,
  And low from sight and cold more close doe keepe.

Then on your Lines you may haue store of Lead,
And bigger Corkes of any size you will,
And where the Fish are vsed to be fed
There shall you lay vpon the bottom still,
And whether that your bayte be Corne, or bread,
Or Wormes, or Paste, it doth not greatly skill,
  For these alone are to be vsed then,
  Vntil the spring or summer come againe.

Thus haue I shew'd how Fish of diuers kinde
Best taken are, and how their bayts to know ;
But *Phœbus* now beyond the westerne *Inde* :
Beginneth to descend and draweth low,
And well the weather serues and gentle winde
Downe with the tide and pleasant streame to row,
  Vnto some place where we may rest vs in,
  Vntill we shall another time begin.

The end of the second Book.

THE THIRD BOOK.

NOW fals it out in order to declare,
What time is best to *Angle* in aright;
And when the chiefe and fittest seasons are
Wherein the fish are most dispos'd to bite,
What winde doth make, and which againe doth marre,
The *Anglers* sport, wherein he takes delight,
    And how he may with pleasure best aspire,
    Vnto the wished end of his desire.

For there are times in which they will not bite,
But doe forbeare and from their foode refraine,
And dayes there are wherein they more delight
To labour for the same and bite amaine;
So, he that can those seasons finde aright
Shall not repent his trauell spent in vaine,
    To walke a mile or two amidst the fields,
    Reaping the fruit this harmlesse pleasure yeelds.

And as a ship in safe and quiet roade
Vnder some hill or harbour doth abide,
With all her fraight, her tackling, and her load,
Attending still the winde and wished tide,
Which when it serues, no longer makes aboad,
But forth into the watry deepe doth slide,
    And through the waues diuides her fairest way
    Vnto the place where she intends to stay.

So must the *Angler* be prouided still,
Of diuers tooles, and sundry baytes in store ;
And all things else pertaining to his skill,
Which he shall get and lay vp long before,
That when the weather frameth to his will,
Hee may be well appointed euermore
   To take fit time when it is offered euer,
   For time in one estate abideth neuer.

THE QUALITIES OF AN ANGLER.

Bvt ere I further goe, it shall behoue
To shew what gifts and qualities of minde
Belongs to him that doth this pastime loue ;
And what the vertues are of euery kinde
Without the which it were in vaine to proue,
Or to expect the pleasure he should finde,
   No more than he that hauing store of meate
   Hath lost all lust and appetite to eate.

For what auails to Brooke or Lake to goe,
With handsome Rods and Hookes of diuers sort,
Well twisted Lines, and many trinkets moe,
To finde the Fish within their watry fort,
If that the minde be not contented so,
But wants great gifts that should the rest support.
   And make his pleasure to his thoughts agree,
   With these therefore he must endued be.

The first is Faith, not wauering and vnstable,
But such as had that holy *Patriarch* old,
That to the highest was so acceptable
As his increase and of-spring manifolde
Exceeded far the starres innumerable,
So must he still a firme perswasion holde,
   That where as waters, brookes, and lakes are found,
   There store of Fish without all doubt abound.

For nature that hath made no emptie thing,
But all her workes doth well and wisely frame,
Hath fild each Brooke, each Riuer, Lake and Spring
With creatures, apt to liue amidst the same;
Euen as the earth, the ayre, and seas doe bring
Forth Beasts, and Birds of sundry sort and name,
  And giuen them shape, ability, and sence,
  To liue and dwell therein without offence.

The second gift and qualitie is Hope,
The anchor-holde of euery hard desire;
That hauing at the day so large a scope,
He shall in time to wished hap aspire,
And ere the Sunne hath left the heau'nly cope,
Obtaine the sport and game he doth desire,
  And that the Fish though sometime slow to bite,
  Will recompence delay with more delight.

The third is Loue, and liking to the game,
And to his friend and neighbour dwelling by;
For greedy pleasure not to spoile the same,
Nor of his Fish some portion to deny
To any that are sicklie, weake, or lame,
But rather with his Line and Angle try
  In Pond or Brooke, to doe what in him lyes,
  To take such store for them as may suffice.

Then followeth Patience, that the furious flame
Of Choller cooles, and Passion puts to flight,
As doth a skilfull rider breake and tame,
The Courser wilde, and teach him tread aright:
So patience doth the minde dispose and frame,
To take mishaps in worth, and count them light,
  As losse of Fish, Line, Hooke, or Lead, or all,
  Or other chance that often may befall.

H

The fift good guift is low Humilitie,
As when a lyon coucheth for his pray
So must he stoope or kneele vpon his knee,
To saue his line or put the weedes away,
Or lye along sometime if neede there be,
For any let or chance that happen may,
    And not to scorne to take a little paine,
    To serue his turne his pleasure to obtaine.

The sixt is painefull strength and courage good,
The greatest to incounter in the Brooke,
If that be happen in his angry mood,
To snatch your bayte, and beare away your Hooke.
With wary skill to rule him in the Flood
Vntill more quiet, tame, and milde he looke,
    And all aduentures constantly to beare,
    That may betide without mistrust or feare.

Next vnto this is Liberalitie,
Feeding them oft with full and plenteous hand,
Of all the rest a' needfull qualitie,
To draw them neere the place where you will stand,
Like to the ancient hospitalitie,
That sometime dwelt in *Albions* fertile land,
    But now is sent away into exile,
    Beyond the bounds of *Issabellas* Ile.

The eight is knowledge how to finde the way
To make them bite when they are dull and slow,
And what doth let the same and breedes delay,
And euery like impediment to know,
That keepes them from their foode and wanted pray,
Within the streame, or standing waters low,
    And with experience skilfully to proue,
    All other faults to mend or to remoue.

The ninth is placabilitie of minde,
Contented with a reasonable dish,
Yea though sometimes no sport at all he finde,
Or that the weather proue not to his wish.
The tenth is thankes to that God, of each kinde,
To net and bayt doth send both foule and Fish,
   And still reserue inough in secret store,
    To please the rich, and to relieue the poore.

Th' eleauenth good guift and hardest to indure,
Is fasting long from all superfluous fare,
Vnto the which he must himselfe inure,
By exercise and vse of dyet spare,
And with the liquor of the waters pure,
Acquaint himselfe if he cannot forbeare,
   And neuer on his greedy belly thinke,
    From rising sunne vntill a low he sincke.

The twelth and last of all is memory,
Remembring well before he setteth out,
Each needfull thing that he must occupy,
And not to stand of any want in doubt,
Or leaue something behinde forgetfully :
When he hath walkt the fields and brokes about,
   It were a griefe backe to retvrne againe,
    For things forgot that should his sport maintaine.

Here then you see what kind of quallities,
An *Angler* should indued be with all,
Besides his skill and other properties,
To serue his turne, as to his lot doth fall :
But now what season for this exercise,
The fittest is and which doth serue but small,
   My Muse vouchsafe some little ayd to lend,
    To bring this also to the wished end.

SEASON AND TIME NOT TO ANGLE.

First, if the weather be to dry and hot,
And scalds with scorching heate the lowly plaine,
As if that youthfull *Phaeton* had got,
The guiding of his fathers Carre againe,
Or that it seem'd *Apollo* had forgot
His light foote steedes to rule with stedfast raine,
     It is not good with any line or Hooke,
     To Angle then in riuer, pond, or brooke.

Or when cold *Boreas* with frosty beard,
Lookes out from vnderneath the lesser beare,
And makes the weary trauailer afeard,
To see the valleys couered euery where
With Ice and Snow, that late so greene appear'd,
The waters stand as if of steele they weare:
     And hoary frosts doe hange on euery bough,
     Where freshest leaues of summer late did grow.

So neither if *Don Æolus* lets goe,
His blustring windes out of the hollow deepe
Where he their strife and strugling to and fro
With triple forke doth still in order keepe,
They rushing forth doe rage with tempests so,
As if they would the world togither sweepe,
     And ruffling so with sturdy blasts they blow,
     That tree and house sometimes they ouer throw.

Besides when shepheards and the swaines repare,
Vnto the brookes with all their flockes of sheepe,
To wash their fleeces and to make them faire,
In euery poole and running water deepe,
The sauour of the wooll doth so impaire,
The pleasant streames, and plunging that they keepe,
     As if that *Lethe*-floud ran euerywhere,
     Or bitter *Doris* intermingled were.

Or when land flouds through long and sudden raine,
Discending from the hills and higher ground,
The sand and mud the cristall streames doe staine,
And make them rise aboue their wonted bound,
To ouer flow the fields and neighbour plaine,
The fruitfull soyle and Meadowes faire are drownd,
      The husbandman doth leese his grasse and hay,
      The bankes their trees, and bridges borne away.

So when the leaues begin to fall apace,
And bough and braunch are naked to be seene,
While nature doth her former worke deface,
Vnclothing bush, and tree, of summers greene,
Whose scattered spoiles lye thicke in euery place,
As sands on shore or starres the poles betweene,
      And top and bottome of the riuers fill,
      To Angle then I also thinke it ill.

All windes are hurtfull if too hard they blow,
The worst of all is that out of the East,
Whose nature makes the Fish to biting slow,
And lets the pastime most of all the rest;
The next that comes from countries clad with Snow,
And *Artique* pole is not offensiue least,
      The Southern winde is counted best of all,
      Then, that which riseth where the sunne doth fall.

BEST TIMES AND SEASONS TO ANGLE.

Bvt if the weather stedfast be and cleare,
Or ouercast with clouds; so it be dry,
And that no signe nor token there appeare,
Of threatning storm through all the empty skie,
But that the ayre is clame and voide of feare,
Of ruffling windes or raging tempests hie,
      Or that with milde and gentle gale they blow,
      Then it is good vnto the brooke to goe.

And when the flouds are fall'n and past away,
And carried haue the dregges into the deepe,
And that the waters waxe more thin and gray,
And leaue their bankes aboue them high and steepe,
The milder streame of colour like to whay,
Within his bounds his wonted course doth keepe,
  And that the wind South or else by-West,
  To Angle then is time and seasons best.

When faire *Aurora* rising early shewes
Her blushing face beyond the Easterne hils,
And dyes the heauenly vault with purple rewes
That far abroad the world with brightnes fils,
The Meadowes greene are hoare with siluer dewes,
That on the earth the sable night distills,
  And chanting birds with merry notes bewray,
  The neere approaching of the chearefull day.

Then let him goe to Riuer, Brooke, or Lake,
That loues the sport, where store of Fish abound,
And through the pleasant fields his iourney make,
Amid'st sweet Pastures, Meadowes fresh and sound,
Where he may best his choice of pastime take,
While swift *Hyperion* runnes his circle round;
  And as the place shall to his liking proue,
  There still remaine or further else remoue.

TO KNOW EACH FISHES HAUNT.

Now that the *Angler* may the better know
Where he may finde each Fish he doth require,
Since some delight in waters still and slow,
And some doe loue the Mud and slimy mire;
Some others where the streame doth swifter flow,
Some stony ground, and grauell some desire,
  Here shall he learne how èuery sort doe seeke,
  To haunt the Layre that doth his nature like.

Carpe, *Eele*, and *Tench*, doe loue a muddie ground,
Eeles vnder stones or hollow rootes doe lye ;
The *Tench* among thicke weedes is soonest found,
The fearfull *Carpe* into the deepe doth flie,
Bream, *Chub* and *Pike*, where clay and sand abound,
Pike loues great pooles, and places full of frie :
　　　The *Chub* delights in streame or shadie tree,
　　　And tender *Breame* in broadest lake to be.

The *Salmon* swift the Riuers sweet doth like,
Where largest streames into the Sea are led :
The spotted *Trout* the smaller Brookes doth seeke,
And in the deepest hole there hides his head :
The prickled *Pearch* in euery hollow creeke,
Hard by the banke, and sandy shoare is fed.
　　　Pearch, *Trout*, and *Salmon* loue cleere waters all,
　　　Greene weedy rockes, and stony grauell small.

So doth the *Bulhead*, *Goodgion*, and the *Loache*,
The most in shallow Brookes delight to be,
The *Ruffe*, the *Dace*, the *Barbill*, and the *Roach*,
Grauell and sand doe loue in lesse degree,
But to the deepe and shade doe more approach,
And ouerhead some couert loue to see,
　　　Of spreading *Poplar*, Oake or Willow greene,
　　　Where vnderneath they lurke for beeing seene.

The mighty *Luce* great waters haunts alway,
And in the stillest place thereof doth lye,
Saue when he raungeth foorth to seeke his pray,
And swift among the feerefull fish doth flye,
The dainty *Humber* loues the marley clay,
And cleerest streames of champion countrie hye,
　　　And in the chiefest pooles thereof doth rest,
　　　Where he is soonest found and taken best.

The *Chauender* amidst the waters fayre,
The swiftest streames doth most himselfe bestow,
The *Shad* and *Tweat* doe rather like the laire,
Of brackish waues, where it doth ebbe and flow,
And thither also doth the flocke repaire,
And flat vpon the bottom lyeth low,
     The *Peele*, the *Mullet*, and the *Suant* good
     Doe like the same, and therein seeke their food.

Bvt here experience doth my skill exceed,
Since diuers Countries diuers Riuers haue;
And diuers Riuers change of waters breed,
And change of waters sundry Fish doth craue,
And sundry Fish in diuers places feede,
As best doth like them in the liquid waue,
     So that by vse and practise may be knowne,
     More then by art or skill can well be showne.

So then it shall be needlesse to declare,
What sundry kindes there lie in secret store,
And where they doe resort, and what they are,
That may be still discouered more and more:
Let him that list no paine or trauell spare
To seeke them out, as I haue done before,
     And then it shall not discontent his minde,
     New choice of place, and change of game to find.

THE BEST HOURES OF THE DAY TO ANGLE.

From first appearing of the rising Sunne,
Till nine of clocke low vnder water best
The Fish will bite, and then from nine to noone,
From noone to foure they doe refraine and rest,
From foure againe till *Phœbus* swift hath runne,
His daily course, and setteth in the West:
     But at the flie aloft they vse to bite,
     All summer long from nine till it be night.

Now least the *Angler* leaue his Tooles behinde,
For lacke of heed or haste of his desire,
And so inforced with vnwilling minde,
Must leaue his game and bacle again retire,
Such things to fetch as there he cannot finde
To serue his turne when neede shall most require,
  Here shall he haue to helpe his memory,
  A .lesson short of euery wants supply.

Light Rod to strike, long line to reach withall,
Strong hooke to holde the fish he haps to hit,
Spare Lines and Hookes, what euer chance doe fall,
Baites quicke and dead to bring them to the bit,
Fine Lead and Quils with Corks both great and small,
Knife, File and thred, and little Basket fit,
  Plummets to sound the depth of clay and sand,
  With Pole and Net to bring them safe to land.

And now we are ariued at the last,
In wished harbour where we meane to rest;
And make an end of this our iourney past:
Here then in quiet roade I thinke it best
We strike our sailes and stedfast Anchor cast
For now the Sunne low setteth in the West,
  And yee *Boat-Swaines*, a merry *Carroll* sing,
  To him that safely did vs hither bring.

FINIS.

*W*OULDST *thou catch Fish?*
    Then here's thy wish;
Take this receipt,
To annoynt thy Baite.

Thou that desir'st to fish with Line and Hooke,
Be it in poole, in Riuer, or in Brooke,
To blisse thy baite, and make the Fish to bite:
Loe, here's a meanes, if thou canst hit it right,
Take Gum of life, fine beat, and laid in soake,
In Oyle, well drawne from that which kils the Oake.
Fish where thou wilt, thou shalt haue sport thy fill,
When twenty faile, thou shalt be sure to kill.

                   Probatum.

    It's perfect and good,
    If well vnderstood;
    Else not to be tolde
    For Siluer or Golde.

                B. R.

FINIS.

LONDON: R. CLAY, SONS, AND TAYLOR, PRINTERS.